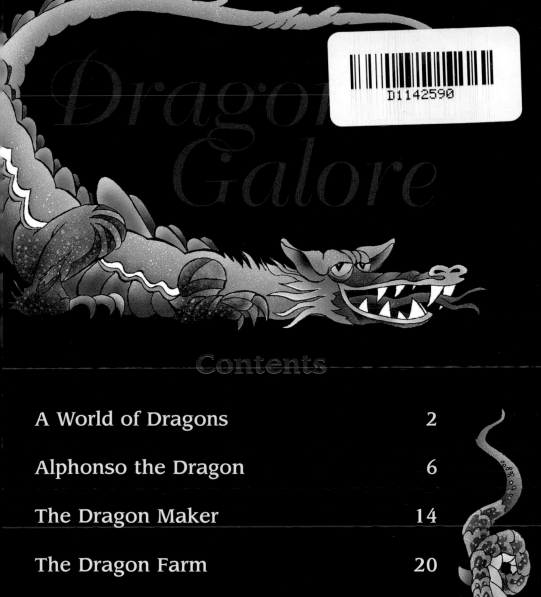

Dragon Galore

Contents

Once upon a time
people said dragons
were real.
They said that
dinosaur bones came
from dragons.

Stories about dragons
are told by people
all over the world.

People said baby dragons
made good pets.

People said that
dragons liked cake.
Cake made the dragons
sleepy.

People said that
dragons had two heads.

People said dragons made rain.
Rain came from sky dragons.

People said food
made dragons happy.

Dragons

Why do you think people tell stories about dragons?

Myths About Dragons

People said. . .

if you ate dragon meat,
you could talk with
the birds!

Dragons did not like bugs.
Bugs could eat dragon brains!

People said that soldiers
came from the teeth
of dragons.

Some people said
that dragons had stones.
The dragons
held the stones in their teeth.
The stones helped the dragons fly.

People said
that dragons could
kill elephants.
The dragons jumped from
trees onto the elephants.

1,000 years

2,000 years

3,000 years

People said that dragons laid eggs.
Baby dragons came out
of the eggs after 3,000 years.

Do you know
what a myth is?

5

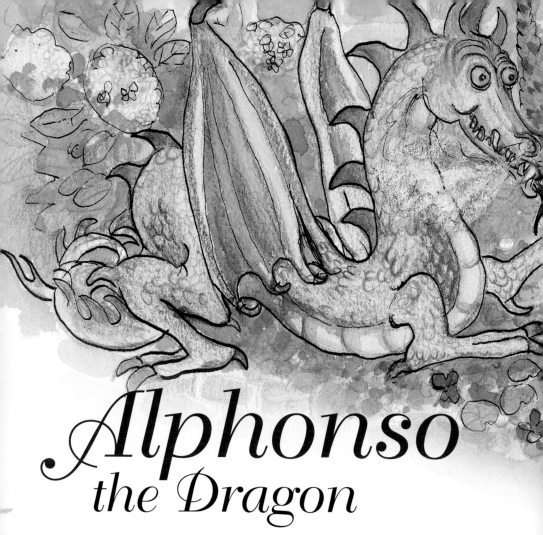

Alphonso
the Dragon

Written by Pauline Cartwright
Illustrated by Linette Porter

Alphonso the dragon came to my garden.
"I am not a big dragon.
I am not a bad dragon,"
Alphonso said.
"I am a small dragon.
I am a kind dragon."

6

"Will you stay in my garden?" I said.

"Yes," said Alphonso.
"I will stay in your garden.
I can go inside, too.
I am an outside-inside kind of dragon.
May I come inside your house?"

"Pat will say no," I said.

What do you think a bad dragon would do?

7

Alphonso was sad.
I got some cake and some cabbage
and some oranges for Alphonso.
He liked the cake.

We played chess in the garden.
"May I come inside your house?"
said Alphonso.

"Dad will say no," I said.
Alphonso was sad.

What game
are they
playing?

8

The sun went away.
It got cold and wet.
Alphonso was still in my garden.
He made little flames.
The little flames made Alphonso hot.
The little flames made me hot, too.

"May I come inside your house?"
said Alphonso.

"Jake will say no," I said.

How long has
Alphonso been in
the garden?

9

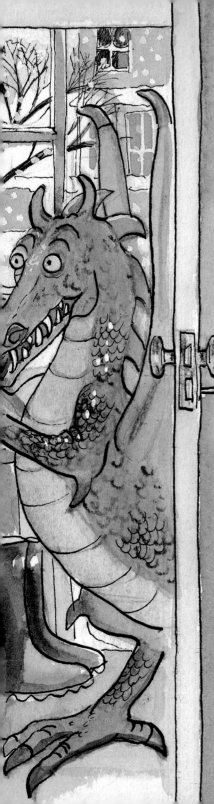

Alphonso was sad.
It got very, very cold.
It snowed and it snowed
and it snowed.

One day,
the lights went off.
The heater went off.
The stove went off.
We were very, very cold.

"What will we do?"
said Dad.

I went into the garden.
I went to get Alphonso.
Alphonso came with me
to the house.

"Oh, no!" said Pat.

"Oh, no!" said Dad.

"Oh, no!" said Jake.
"What is that?"

"A heater," I said.

11

Alphonso came inside.
He made little flames.
The little flames made me hot.
The little flames made Dad hot.
The little flames made Pat hot.
The little flames made Jake hot.

12

How will
this story end?

Alphonso made little flames all day.
That night, the lights came back on.
"Good," I said. "We can play chess."
Pat and Dad and Jake
and Alphonso and I played chess.

"Alphonso is an outside-inside dragon," I said.
"Can he stay inside the house?"

"Yes," said Pat.

"Yes," said Dad.

"Yes," said Jake.
"Alphonso is our outside-inside dragon."

The Dragon Maker

Brian Stewart loves dragons.
He makes dragons.
He is a dragon maker.
Brian makes dragons from clay.
Some dragons are big.
Some dragons are small.
Some dragons have
their own names.

Can you think of some names for these dragons?

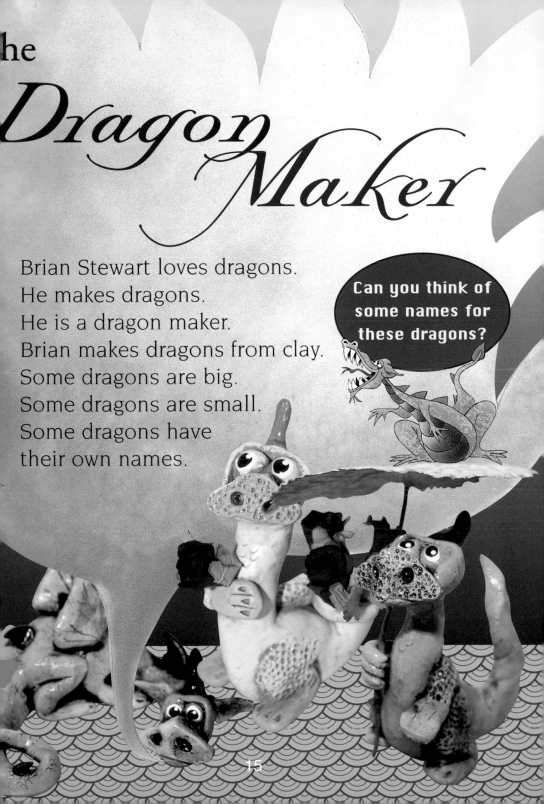

Making a Dragon

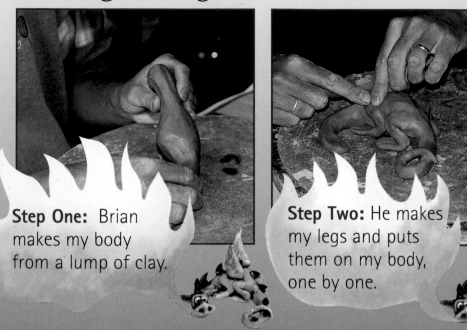

Step One: Brian makes my body from a lump of clay.

Step Two: He makes my legs and puts them on my body, one by one.

Slip (a mix of clay and water) sticks my legs and my head and wings to my body. With no slip, I could break up when I am baked in the kiln, or the oven.

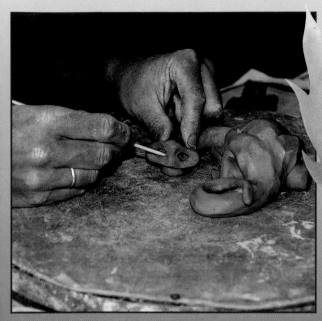

Step Three: My head is fixed to my body and Brian makes my nose. He uses a long metal rod.

Step Four: My eyes are put on. Now I look like a real dragon! The hood over my eyes is fixed on with more slip.

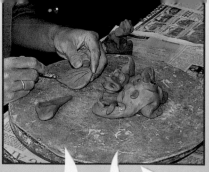

Step Five: Brian makes my wings and spikes. He puts them on my body.

Step Six: Now the scales. The scales are made by a straw. The straw stamps a pattern of scales all over my body. Awesome!

Step Seven: Brian gives me two weeks to dry. Then I go into the kiln. (If I am not dry, I would blow up in there!) Inside the kiln, I bake for eighteen hours. It's hot in there, even in dragon talk!

Step Eight: I get taken from the kiln and I am painted. Soon, I will find a home with a new dragon lover.

Could you tell a friend how to make a dragon?

The Dragon Farm

Written by Judy Ling
Illustrated by Philip Webb

The Dragon Farm
*is a story with more than
one storyteller.
You will find out how
a story changes from
storyteller to storyteller!*

21

The dragons went to look for a farm.

24

Farmer Green liked her dragon farm.
"You are good dragons," she said.
"You stay inside the wall and eat grass."

Farmer Brown and Farmer Black
did not like the dragons.

They will not be good for long.

What bad things could dragons do?

Farmer Brown and Farmer Black were right.
Soon the dragons ate up . . .

. . . all the grass,

. . . all the trees,

. . . and all the flowers.

They made big flames at night to keep away the dark.
And they roared and they roared and they roared.

This is no good! Those dragons will have to go back to Scungy Swamp.

Will they go back to Scungy Swamp? What do you think?

Farmer Green did not want
to take the dragons back
to Scungy Swamp.
She made a list:

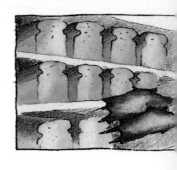

"This is no good," she said.
"The dragons have to go
back to Scungy Swamp."

The dragons did not want to go
back to Scungy Swamp.
They had a meeting.
They made a list.

What
else could the
dragons do?

"This is good," they said.
"Now we will not have to go
back to Scungy Swamp!"

The dragons helped the baker bake the bread.

The dragons helped the potter bake the clay.

The dragons helped the pilots land the planes.

The dragons helped the people heat the houses.
They were very, very, very good.

The people liked the dragons helping.
"Do not make the dragons go back
to Scungy Swamp!" they said.

So the dragons stayed with Farmer Green
and everyone was happy."

WILDCATS
Lion

Glossary

- **chess** – a board game, with pieces called chessmen, that is played by two people

- **clay** – an earth, used to make pots and models

- **dragon** – a make-believe monster with wings and claws (said to sometimes breathe fire)

- **hood** – a fold of skin that looks like a hood on the head of a dragon

- **myth** – a story told throughout the years about superhuman beings or about how something came to be

- **scales** – the thin flat plates that cover the body of a dragon

- **slip** – a mixture of clay and water

- **swamp** – a place where the ground is usually wet and spongy